BEAR UP
Bear Ways to Cope with Life's Bumps and Surprises

Jane and Mimi Noland

Drawings by Mimi Noland

CompCare® Publishers
3850 Annapolis Lane, Suite 100
Minneapolis, Minnesota 55447-5443

Library of Congress Cataloging-in-Publication Data

Noland, Jane Thomas.
         Bear Up: Bear Ways to Cope with Life's Bumps and
         Surprises./Jane and Mimi Noland
                      p.cm.
ISBN: 0-89638-323-7: $6.95
1. Bears–Humor. I. Noland, Mimi, 1959-   II. Title.
PN6231.B42N64 1993
818 .5402–dc20   93-27109

Cover design by MacLean & Tuminelly

Inquiries, orders, and catalog requests should be addressed to:
CompCare Publishers
3850 Annapolis Lane, Suite 100
Minneapolis, Minnesota 55447-5443
Call toll free 800/328-3330
or 612/559-4800

To Dick Noland, husband, father, mentor,
whose constant creativity carries us
to heady pinnacles of humor.

And to the Goodbears themselves,
who, modeled after American black bears,
have taken on a very real identity of their own,
as wise (most of the time), dignified,
and down-to-earth funny.

Bearing Up

The Goodbears (good bears always trying to be better bears) were introduced in *Bearables, Parables of Bear Wisdom for Everyday Living*. Now, to all humans willing to listen and learn, *Bear Up* brings more practical wisdom from the world of bears.

Bears have always been known for their amazing adaptability and for a chin-up attitude in the face of disaster. (Why else would *bear up* be such a well-used term of encouragement among English-speaking humans?) Whatever happens to the Goodbears—from rock slides to bearnappings, county fairs to flour sacks, dynamite blasts to dump closings—they handle with an enviable degree of resiliency.

Resiliency. For bears and humans alike, that's what gets us through our challenges and rocky times. The Goodbears, credentialed as they are in survival skills, may be the very best teachers humans can find in the ancient art of bearing up.

The little stories in this book, as in *Bearables*, come straight out of bear country and are based on real bear behavior. The drawings translate these lessons—or bearables—into maxims useful to humans. Here, Serena Goodbear, model of motherhood and upstanding example of *Ursus americanus*, goes about her bear business: parenting, nonstop dining, and taking incredibly long naps. To her succession of rowdy cubs, she teaches time-tested bear ways of coping with life's bumps and surprises.

Know Your Goodbears

Serena, sow supreme, a fountain of bear wisdom.

Dunbar, big boar and respected fisherbear, father of Dubu and Serendipity (Dipity), Serena's youngest cubs.

Bjorn, Serena's firstborn, off somewhere being a male.

Flora, Fauna, and Fedora, Serena's rainbow triplets, pursued by paparazzi in their cubhood because each is a slightly different color.

Kuma and Ursula, Serena's older twins, still around getting into trouble.

Dubu, a lovable little clown, and his sister Dipity, bright, lucky, a female jock.

Aunt Arctica, Serena's sister.

Oso, one of Aunt Arctica's older cubs, an adolescent bear burglar, known for breaking and entering cabins and helping humans unload grocery bags. He vanished after visiting a camp lodge, dipping into the sugar bowls and trying to pry up the lid on the bun-warmer while sitting on it (a gymnastic feat).

Irving, Serena's brother, who lost his identity in an avalanche.

Superior, Serena's mother.

Savoir Bear, a hermit bear, who lives—and is—over the hill. Long past the rivalries of his studding days, he's open to sharing his wisdom, along with his blueberries.

Dave, a musclebear, Serena's passing fancy.

Assorted cousins, aunts, uncles, and shirt-tail relatives.

(Of course, these are names assigned by humans. Who knows what the Goodbears call themselves? Untranslated, their names may be rich with throaty German consonants or rolling Scottish R's, creative combinations of bear sounds—hums, moans, coughs, snorts, sniffs, whuffles, woofs, and stereotypical growls.)

A Morning Jolt

April rolled around again, shrinking the last patches of snow in the shadiest deeps of the forest. It was rise-and-shine time for Serena, supermom and source of bear wisdom, and her year-old cubs, Dubu, the clown, and Serendipity (Dipity for short), the lucky.

Bears, especially grown-up ones, are not inclined to bounce out of bed after a winter-long nap. Serena was no exception. On the other hand, Dubu and Dipity, who woke up earlier, were full of beans and raring to go.

Like young ones the world over, who pounce on their sleeping parents at dawn on Saturday mornings demanding cereal and services, Dubu and Dipity poked at Serena. They made restless "c'mon, Mom, get up" noises.

Eventually maternal instinct won over self-indulgence (as it generally does with bears). Serena dragged herself, groggy and rumpled, from their winter quarters under the toes of a fallen oak.

She was not as totally charmed by her cubs as she had been when they were tiny. But her yearlings, Dubu and Dipity, exuberantly checking out the familiarities of their forest home with eyes, ears, paws, and muzzles, *were* enchanting. Serena got over her irritation in a hurry at the sight of such youthful joie de vivre.

A cure for grumpiness: observe the antics of youth.

When your offspring are too much for you, concentrate on their endearing qualities.

A cure for grumpiness: observe the antics of youth.

When your offspring are too much for you,
concentrate on their endearing qualities.

The Spring Bind

When Serena first made her appearance in the spring, she was not her usual matter-of-fact, focused self. She was even a little withdrawn. Truth was, she was preoccupied with a health matter: she was plugged up. Hardly an unexpected problem when you've been living in a den without facilities for six months and your digestive system has been shut down (conveniently).

Without a handy supply of Metamucil, Serena headed straight for the place where cascara (nature's broom) and other green herbs grew. She knew, instinctively and precisely, which herbs and grasses made up her spring tonic. She munched a mixture of them, then pointed them out with her muzzle to Dubu and Dipity.

The natural remedy worked fine. A group of hikers along the old lumber trail could attest—with shrieks—to that.

Serena felt much perkier now. She was ready, empty, and eager for summer's banquet.

For ordinary ills, try nature's remedies first.

For ordinary ills, try nature's remedies first.

Shrinking Territory

When Serena, with Dipity and Dubu trailing along, made the spring tour of her territory, she was baffled. Where were the landmarks—the bear trees she had clawed to lay claim to this spot? Where was her favorite blueberry patch? Her entire western boundary had been altered. What had been forest with a few sunny clearings was now a stretch of highway blacktop. The gentle rustles and cheeps of the woods had been replaced by waves of whizzing traffic.

Serena shook her big head, as if to clear away the sight of this ugly (to a bear) reality. Dubu and Dipity were disoriented too. Their homeland had shrunk visibly since last summer's geography lessons.

Serena had two alternatives: to push her boundaries to the south—and infringe on another sow's homestead—or to make do with less acreage. Serena chose the first. Aunt Arctica had established herself on the southern territory. And since Arctica was rather passive, as bears go (although hardly a pushover), Serena could avoid any confrontation more serious than a sisterly spat.

With a sigh (the sniffing equivalent of "Oh, botheration!"), Serena set out to revise her boundaries and claim squatter's rights along the property line.

Know when to negotiate.

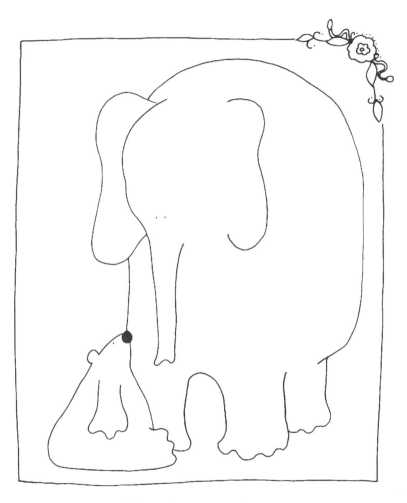

Know when to negotiate.

A Rock Slide

Serena could not read the highway sign BEWARE OF FALLING ROCK. (For humans, who could, the sign never helped much anyway; by the time they were close enough to read it, the rock they were supposed to beware of was already falling!) But even without road signs, Serena was wary of rock slides. Her uneasiness harked back to an incident in her cubhood.

Early in their second summer, she and her brother and sister trailed after their mother, Superior, across the top of a cliff—rust and black-gray jags of rock bleeding silvery rivulets after a rainstorm. The cliff slanted into a curve of the highway above the big lake.

Superior, still punchy from her winter's nap, was unaware that the rain had begun to loosen some sizable rocks from their red-earth beds. Her big pawsteps finished the job. As the ground gave way behind Superior, Serena and her sister tumbled—but not far. They scrambled back up. No harm done, except for one rock that landed wickedly on Serena's leftmost toe. (Even now, when the weather turned damp, a toe-twinge could conjure up an avalanche in Serena's memory.)

Their brother was not so lucky. He went slithering and bouncing down the cliff along with some sharp-edged boulders. By the time Superior could lead her other two around and down to the foot of the cliff, he had vanished. They looked, but never found him. Superior, dejected over the lost cub, finally pulled herself together and gave an extra dose of motherly attention to Serena and her sister, Arctica.

But Serena never forgot the ominous rumble of that rock slide. Later, when she had cubs of her own, she never led them too close to the top of the cliff. Instead, she started them out lower— on the rock wall loosely built by humans to keep the lake from biting into the meadow. Here, in this safer place, her cubs learned from pinched toes and bruised bottoms to fear the sound and feel of rocks shifting under their feet.

**If you feel like mothering,
there's always someone who needs it.**

**Keep an ear out for rumbles,
especially in high places.**

If you feel like mothering,
there's always someone who needs it.

Keep an ear out for rumbles,
especially in high places.

Change of Identity

Two young humans—brothers—in the back of a van rounding the highway bend saw him first, a black cub, stunned and sitting in a ravine just before the cliff projected into the curve.

"Lookit the BEAR in our ravine! Can't we stop?" said one. It wasn't "their" ravine, but they claimed it anyway, since their summer cabin was within yelling distance and they'd spent hours hoohooing into it to retrieve the echoes.

"Heavens, no, not here!" said the boys' mother from the driver's seat.

As the van slowed for the curve, the older boy—even though he'd been warned about feeding bears—sneakily threw a half-eaten Big Mac in the cub's direction.

The cub had a cut and a headache—maybe a concussion—from his slide down the cliff. But the smell of the burger enticed him out of his funk. Headache or not, he got up and went for it.

"His name is Irving," announced the burger-tosser.

"Yeah," said his brother.

"Why not?" said their mother.

They stopped down the road at a log gift shop and told the shopowner about "Irving in our ravine."

"We can take care of him," said the shopowner, who kept a little zoo behind his shop—deer, llamas, pygmy goats, two peacocks, and one bear cub in a pit.

So Irving was picked up, stitched by a vet, and put into the metal-sided pit with the other cub. He was fed well. He also accepted with grace any empty cones—gifts from human parents and kids who came to peer at the pacing cubs.

In no time, Irving forgot Superior's lessons on how to be a woods bear. Instead, he would be a zoo bear, transported to a real zoo in the fall. There he became an actor, taking on alternately cute or gruff roles (depending on his mood) against a simulated forest backdrop—hardly the pursuit nature had intended. Oh, well—a bear in unnatural circumstances almost always looks for a silver lining. At least zookeepers wouldn't make him dance to a hurdygurdy!

**Never underestimate
the healing power of food.**

**If you lose your identity,
find a new one.**

Never underestimate
the healing power of food.

If you lose your identity,
find a new one.

Blasts

An explosion shocked the Goodbears' forest. A huge, echoing blast. Then another. And another. Birds teetered on their pine perches. Browsing deer froze into statues. Even the Goodbears, who were pretty calm about most things, stopped cold and stood up on their back legs to sniff out the origin of such booms. Inside humans' cabins, framed photos tilted on their picture hooks, and people made awed noises like "Wow!" or "That was a real rocker!"

Serena Goodbear and her cubs were close enough to the road to see that a new human community had sprung up over the winter—an office trailer, a bulldozer, a crane, heaps of sand, a loading hopper, and a parade of cement trucks. An enormous, arched, black hole had appeared in the face of the rock. Where the hole wasn't, the cliff was draped in heavy woven wire to contain falling rocks. One sign informed human passersby what all this meant: YOUR HIGHWAY TAXES AT WORK—at work dynamiting a tunnel to reroute the road along the shore.

Serena, if she had been made of less stubborn stuff, might have packed up Dipity and Dubu and left, taking her chances on acquiring a corner of a neighbor bear's territory. But it would take more than dynamite to move *this* mama from *her* forest.

A believer in the lemonade-from-lemons approach, Serena noticed that the blasts vibrating the forest floor actually rattled some rodents (protein tidbits) out of their earth chambers. It wasn't every day that Serena had the chance to teach her cubs the finer points of mouse hunting! From a bear's point of view, even dynamite was not all bad.

Make the best of misfortune.

One creature's ease is another's discomfort.

Make the best of misfortune.

One creature's ease is another's discomfort.

Encounters of the Sharpest Kind

When Ursula, an older sister of the Dipity-Dubu pair, was first getting acquainted on her own with the inhabitants of the forest, she came upon a little hunched-up animal who looked as if he had a bad haircut, as well as bad posture.

Overcome with curiosity, Ursula took a long time to sniff at this disheveled being. Too long. For suddenly her muzzle stung, then felt heavy with barbs of pain. Through an oversight, Serena had not clued in Ursula on porcupines, their short fuses and the arsenals in their backpacks. One thing *was* lucky; the porcupine was young too (although considerably more mature for his age than Ursula), and he aimed wild. Most of his quiverful stuck in a nearby bank, and Ursula was left prickling with just a few quills around her nose.

The encounter, though painful, might have been a lot worse.

**Avoid provoking anyone
who is known to be prickly.**

Avoid provoking anyone
who is known to be prickly.

Surprises

As a parent, Serena was conscientious and exacting. A human-parent maxim, such as "Look both ways before you cross the street," in bear-parent talk (mostly huffs and snuffles and an occasional woof) becomes even more thorough: "Look up, down, sideways, and backwards before you make a move, no matter where you are. And if you sniff danger, hie your little furry selves up the nearest tree."

She tried (as mother bears do) to cover every eventuality. But who could predict that Dubu, sniffing around a dumpster, would have pepper thrown in his face by a red-faced chef? Or that Dipity, doing the same thing, would have to dance over the crackle and smoke of a package of ladyfingers set off at her feet? (Now, most dumpsters, probably for the long-term good of all parties concerned, are ringed by off-putting electric-fence wires.)

Such discouragements related to human food sent Dubu and Dipity back to doing mostly what they needed to do: develop their natural skills—log-rolling (to turn up pupae) and berry-picking.

**Not even a hovering mother
can shield you from surprises.**

Not even a hovering mother
can shield you from surprises.

An Unmotherly Lapse

In spite of the risks involved and the tug of maternal responsibility, sometimes a sow just can't pass up the temptation of human cooking. One golden day, an unusually delightful smell wafted like a beckoning banner into the forest. Not only Dubu, but Serena herself (against her better judgment), followed the ribbon of scent to a cabin porch. There on a table, pale-brown and sugary and oozing apple filling, was a fresh-baked pie.

Serena's resistance was low. She'd had a fretful morning, trying to keep both cubs from bolting across the road and into another mother's realm. Serena was not about to give Dubu first crack at this culinary wonder. To his astonishment, she was not even willing to play sharesy. She marched up the wooden steps, opened the screen door by its handle, and grabbed the pie in her mouth. At the edge of the woods, she turned her back on her son and proceeded to clean the pie out of the pan in a matter of seconds, grrr-ing at him to stand back. All she left him was a disappointing ring of bottom crust.

Serena (as bears do) held many of the same basic values generally ascribed to humans, like motherhood and apple pie—but not necessarily in that order. For a bear on a summer-long binge, apple pie comes first!

**Never let food become an issue
in a relationship.**

Never let food become an issue
in a relationship.

Errors of Youth

Dipity and Dubu teetered on the brink of adolescence. So Serena (as mother bears do) loosened her apron strings and allowed them time each day away from her. She had maternal misgivings, for independence often spelled trouble for young bears trying to find the shaky balance between humans and bears (and bears and bears).

Dipity and Dubu were bound to tangle with humans. A farmer brandishing a garden hoe chased Dubu out of his zucchini. A beekeeper shot at Dipity with a pellet rifle, stinging her rear. Dubu climbed on a window box and turned on an outdoor faucet that shocked him with a geyser. A band of human hikers, singing camp songs, sent both cubs scurrying into hiding beside the trail. An oil truck sped around a turn, ruffling Dubu's fur as he ambled along the shoulder of the highway—a squeak that made his heart pound.

One gentle human, who admitted to his neighbors that Dipity "didn't have a mean bone in her body," nevertheless cut her off from her favorite sunflower seeds by stringing up his birdfeeder on a pulley between two birches. He also slammed a door in her face when she marched onto his deck to appeal her case.

Through all these encounters, Serena stood by, near enough to advise, wise enough to let them learn from their own follies.

Mistakes are the best teachers.

Mistakes are the best teachers.

An Enormous Gull

Brashly returning to the scene of an earlier success (as bears do), Dipity found her way one afternoon to the same clothesline where she had stolen a shag rug to cozy up last winter's den. This time she discovered the fun of hanging on the line, along with a whole sailing-fleet of sheets and pillowcases. The sight of a bear cub happily swinging to and fro with the blowing laundry startled the cabin owner, who dropped her clothes basket and billowed a sheet at Dipity.

All Dipity was aware of was a huge, white seagull—the biggest gull she had ever seen—flapping its wings and rasping out magnified gull sounds at her.

She abandoned her gymnastics and ran like a beachball back to Serena. The lesson was clear: don't swing on clotheslines—or leave pawprints on sheets, either—if you don't want to face oversized, scolding birds.

**You don't always strike up friendships
while hanging out at the gym.**

You don't always strike up friendships
while hanging out at the gym.

A Carnival

A small carnival trucked into town and unloaded on the county fairgrounds: a Ferris wheel, a Tilt-a-Whirl, a Caterpillar, and booths with pitch games and food. Fun for the local kids. Fun for the local bears, who came around at night after the rides ground to a halt and poked around in trash barrels for half-eaten corn dogs and melted rainbow cones.

Kuma and Ursula, Serena's three-year-old twins were among them. Ursula, displaying some of Serena's restraint, found a few goodies in a barrel at the edge and retreated. Kuma ventured farther, snooping first in one barrel, then another, until he discovered (and consumed) a cloud of spun candy on the floor of the Caterpillar. There, under the Caterpillar cover, he fell asleep.

Morning came, along with carnies barking out the wonders of their rides. Kuma sneaked out of the Caterpillar and hid behind a seat on the Tilt-a-Whirl, just as the barker started it up as a lure for ticket-buyers. The terrified Kuma was spun into action and flung everywhichway, until he climbed onto a whirling, dipping seat and gripped it for dear life.

At the sight of his furry passenger, the equally terrified ridemaster (from Atlanta) shut down the ride. Bear and barker bolted in opposite directions. Kuma headed full bore for the nearest woods, his innards churning. He couldn't tell if *he* had caused the awful, screeching din, or if it was just the normal sound of human fun. But the carnival lights and shouts, the whirs and grinds—even the food—lost appeal for him, not only for that moment, but forever more.

Fun can be very scary.

Don't stay too long at the fair.

Fun can be very scary.

Don't stay too long at the fair.

Scarebears

Dipity was lost. She looked for Serena high (on rock promontories and on leaning trees) and low (in the meadows near the lake). Once Dipity was sure she saw her, but in a most unlikely place—next to a bungalow in town. She saw a procession of black bears quietly nibbling the lawn, heads down, all facing the same direction. This had to be Serena, with Aunt Arctica and her cubs.

Dipity went closer, to where she could whine a lost-cub sound and expect an answer. But Serena and Aunt Arctica never looked up. Dipity moved to another vantage and discovered something peculiar: when viewed from the side, these bears were very thin—plywood thin. And from back in the woods the real Serena was harumphing to her. Dipity had been duped.

If these two-dimensional bears were scarebears, intended to keep bears away, the humans who put them there were unaware that they might, instead, *attract* bears. For, as bears' neighbors know, not all bears are loners. Mothers often hang out with other sociable sows and bear-sit each others' offspring. Who knows what curious bear might see the likeness of some chum or relative or old flame in one of these lawn figures and come to check it out?

For craftsy humans, the painted plywood bears—along with sunbonneted cherubs tipping watering cans and upended gardeners displaying their bloomers—were simply lawn art. Nobody meant to confuse a real bear, like Dipity.

It's not always easy to differentiate between life and art.

Don't get taken in by fakes.

It's not always easy to differentiate
between life and art.

Don't get taken in by fakes.

A Hole and a Fall

Dubu, chasing butterflies one late afternoon in a sun-spotted glade he remembered from the summer before, fell smack into a huge hole that he did *not* remember. No wonder. The place had become the construction site of some human's den. And Dubu, who was inclined to be a klutz (he'd fallen out of a tree more than once), stepped off a concrete-block wall into the unfinished basement. Anxiously he went from one wall to another, scraping for a claw-grip. He even tried hopping up, but bears, being low in the bottom, are not great jumpers. Dubu was trapped.

As darkness blurred the outlines of things, Dubu moaned out an SOS, over and over, in the hope that Serena would hear. (Dubu was still young enough to believe that mothers had all the answers. In this case, Serena didn't.) She heard him, all right, but there wasn't a thing she could do except pace around the clearing and worry.

Come morning, a truck arrived. A couple of human builders got out and buckled on their tool belts. Serena backed discreetly into the forest, but Dubu had nowhere to hide. He was careful not to look the humans in the eye.

"Well, can you beat this!" said one.

"A yearling," said the other, before posing a question commonly heard in the north country: "I wonder where his mother is. . . ."

The two humans put down a ramp of boards and a ladder. Dubu hugged it and climbed out in ungracious haste.

As he cantered off to find Serena, he thought about bears and humans. Sometimes even a bear has mixed feelings.

Worry is not a solution.

**Help sometimes comes
from an unexpected source.**

Worry is not a solution.

Help sometimes comes
from an unexpected source.

A Denful

Aunt Arctica approached each pregnancy with trepidation. Who wouldn't, after her experience six seasons ago when she woke up with five cubs, all poking and tugging at her simultaneously? Although bears aren't into counting, she would have sworn on a bushel of blueberries that she'd given birth to only two!

Had she only dreamed that she saw a human in a checked shirt invade the privacy of her den on a cold day in February? Had she dreamed that he had placed three extra cubs, gently, one at a time, on her belly before squirming out of the den backwards?

Somnolence kept the facts from her. Truth was, since she was known in bear and human circles alike as a seasoned sow and a dependable mother, she'd been presented by the forestry service with three orphaned cubs to raise along with her own. From her observations, Aunt Arctica was aware that nature could give a bear mother as many as five—even six—cubs when times were prosperous. So quintuplets were not out of the realm of biological possibility.

With a huff of a sigh, she accepted gracefully the extra mouths at her table, although she wore herself to a nub that following summer just keeping track of five tumbling furballs.

Don't get caught napping;
you may be tricked into parenthood.

Once a mother, always a mother.

Don't get caught napping;
you may be tricked into parenthood.

Once a mother, always a mother.

Dilemma

Acorn-colored Flora was a homebody. She had spent three summers in her own treehouse, draped over the branches of a Dago crab in the back yard of a tolerant pair of humans. She strayed just far enough to touch base with her goldish sister Fauna and her reddish brother Fedora.

She had discovered her treehouse when the Dago was in blossom. She couldn't resist, climbed up, and stayed. She felt safe there, day and night. A big human in a red hat used to cluck at her. But when Flora proved she wasn't a nuisance, the human and his wife left her alone. Life was sweet—well, not too sweet, since her diet consisted largely of Dago crabs and an occasional cabbage from the garden. The humans didn't mind. They could eat only so much crab jelly and coleslaw.

Now the human in the red hat was gone. If anyone asked his wife about the tree-bear, she said, simply, "This is her home." Even when winter forced Flora out of her tree, she denned up close by.

Only the threat of spinsterhood lured her out of her high rise. During her fifth summer, an attractive boar whuffled to her from the foot of her tree. When faced with a dilemma—love or security—Flora opted for the former.

But one thing was certain: Flora the homing bear would never go far, and she would always come home for her summer feast of crabapples and cabbages.

**When faced with life choices,
listen to your heart.**

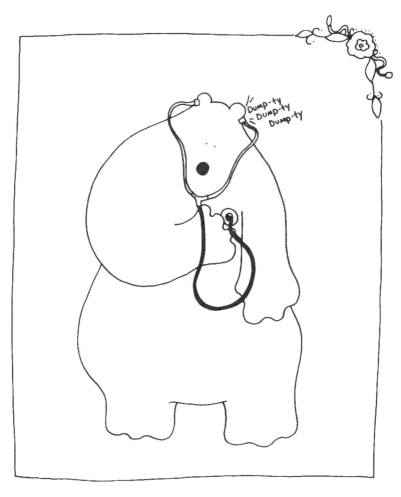

When faced with life choices,
listen to your heart.

The Closing of the Dump

For bears, the closing of a dump is an economic disaster on a par with the Irish Potato Famine or the Great Depression. When Serena, taking an afternoon off from Dubu and Dipity, made her first dump visit of the summer, she found nothing but a mound of gravel. She was undone. The dump had always been a gathering place, like the country store of yore. Generations of bears—and humans, too, encased in their pick-ups and woodies—had met there for conversation over garbage.

For as long as Serena could remember, bears had spiced up their natural diets with human leftovers. Now there would be no more Spaghetti-Os or Arrowroots or petrified marshmallows. Back to dandelions and Botany 101!

Humans, suddenly fearful about their fragile environment, were now carting their rinsed-out, stomped-on cans to the town's recycling center. This ticked off the bears, who have a limited vision of what recycling can do for the long-term good of the planet.

Bears, in general, are very NOW. Even the wisest of the Goodbears espouse consumerism. In protest to the dump-closing, bear activists took to performing drum rolls on garbage cans in back yards and garages.

Serena, wisely, kept her paws out of protests. She faded into the forest with a renewed vow to protect her cubs from bear-human politics.

When civilization fails you,
go back to nature.

Sometimes a change of lifestyle is in order.

When civilization fails you,
go back to nature.

Sometimes a change of lifestyle is in order.

Codependency

A few chosen Goodbears took advantage of one gutsy human who got a kick out of feeding them. Although the practice was frowned upon by naturalists, who believed codependent bears were not healthy for either species, the human had operated a cafeteria for bears since long before bear-feeding was discounted.

Every day the human set out buckets of high-calorie feed and scraps. And every day a few opportunists—the same ones summer after summer—lumbered into his yard to partake. He named them: Bertha, Barbara, Buster, Bowtie (from the white on his chest). These adults were followed by second-seating adolescents, all known as "little tyke." The regulars, aware that they had a soft deal, did not share their secret widely. But one afternoon, Dubu, who always *did* have a nose for treats, happened on the scene. He waited until the big bears wafted off, then dove into a bucket.

Dubu licked up the last leaves of a Caesar salad that larger muzzles had missed. A joy—until he got his head stuck in the bucket. With the dark, rubbery thing clamped on his head, he danced blindly around the yard like some medieval mummer, moaning and huffing. The human, who heard and came to help, wished he hadn't. For, while getting unstuck, Dubu flailed out and raked him. The human spent weeks recovering from his wounds—then went right back to feeding bears. Dubu, free of his bucket helmet, never returned.

Nosiness can become an impediment.

Nosiness can become an impediment.

Changing Times

With the closing of the dump, Serena, adaptable as ever, recognized that times were changing. She enrolled in a Back to Nature seminar (assuming there would be some nature somewhere to go back to) taught by her great-great-uncle, Savoir Bear.

Savoir Bear was a Goodbear elder, a Euell Gibbons among bears. Long past his years as a romantic rogue, he occasionally came lumbering over the crest of the hill to visit the Goodbear matriarchs. In his spent and superannuated state, he put aside male pride and concentrated on developing intellectually and spiritually. Unboarlike, he was okay with hanging out with Serena and her cubs, to whom he passed along his vast knowledge of berries and bugs, roots, herbs, and river life.

Savoir Bear also shared his den-building skills (he was especially good at fortifying secret sleeping places). No creature, human or otherwise, ever stormed *his* snow forts! Even slapdash little Dubu learned from Uncle Savoir that knowledge and planning translate directly into peace of mind.

Remember to tap the wisdom of your elders.

Remember to tap the wisdom of your elders.

A Ghost

A sheriff saw it first: an apparition in the shape of a bear meandering down Main Street, ghostly white under the lumberyard floodlight. The sheriff choked on his doughnut and fired his Remington into the air. This snapped up a few window shades and brought a handful of hardies out onto their stoops. By the time the ghost bear had nosed its way through town, a dozen humans had seen it and bandied about at least as many theories: It was a stray polar bear. It was a Kermode, a lightish bear from British Columbia. It was an albino. It was the spirit of the Ojibwe Maykwa. No, it was an entirely new species—call it *Ursus niveus*.

Morning revealed the truth. Powdery pawprints led out the rear door of the bakery, left open by the new bun-baker from the city, not yet bear-wise. Three huge flour sacks on a shelf had been raked and overturned, presumably dusting the bear from crown to claws with white. The bakery owner, sweeping up the mess, swore it had to be that bandit Oso, although there were those who clung to a more supernatural explanation.

As for Oso himself, he was later airlifted to Michigan. But, as one of a reckless few who fly in the face of conformity, Oso became a folk hero (perhaps even among bears). The tales of his pranks, tall to begin with, grew taller as human raconteurs traded them in the safe glow of their campfires.

**If you're viewed as supernatural,
make the most of it.**

If you're viewed as supernatural,
make the most of it.

The Pain of Independence

Dubu and Dipity were confused. Serena, who had always been there for them, was suddenly aloof, staring over their heads at some fantasy of her own. She was not responding to their beeps for help in ordinary matters. In fact, she seemed to have cooled off to the whole idea of motherhood.

One day, she cuffed Dubu (gently) for getting between her and the object of her interest: a fit male bear who loomed up out of the forest in courting mode. Was it their absentee father, Dunbar? Dubu couldn't tell. Dipity, however, who had learned to fish by observing her father from afar, knew that this was some-one new—an ursine weightlifter named Dave.

Dipity and Dubu were suddenly on their own, while Serena, giddy as a schoolgirl, flounced around with her suitor through the buttercups. Serena knew that the affair would be brief, a couple of weeks. But how affirming it was to her sowhood to set parent-ing aside and savor the companionship—however fleeting—of an adult male!

Once Dave had gone on his roué way, Serena warmed up a bit to her cubs. She at least tolerated their questions and warned them about major faux pas, like falling into the river or eating plants that could give them gollywoggles.

Sometimes even mothers need to feel pretty.

Sometimes even mothers need to feel pretty.

An Economic Slump

Now that the dump had closed and berries were wizened with drought, it was all a mombear could do to gather enough food to make it through winter and another pregnancy. (In a prosperous year, a bear can put away as many as 20,000 calories in a summer day—that's a whole lot of acorns!)

Serena was wiped out from perpetual motherhood. She decided to take a year off. That is, her body decided. Although she'd had her biennial tryst in late June with that wandering hunk of a boar, Dave, the pregnancy just didn't take. For Serena, like others of her sow sisterhood, conceives in June, but doesn't really start working on her pregnancy until late fall, so her cubs will *always* be born in the dead of winter. If she finds slim pickin's on the berry bushes that season—or if she's too skinny for her own good—she may not beget at all. In this case, bears have it all over humans, who seldom wait for fortuitous times; they just barge ahead and procreate willy nilly.

Serena *deserved* a vacation. She might even give Dipity and Dubu another season of attention. They could use it. She didn't want any cub of hers turning out like her nephew Oso the Burglar!

Practice family planning.

Practice family planning.

Civilization

For bears, civilization spells trouble. Towns shrink bears' territories and set them to squabbling among themselves. Resorts in bear country add up no-win, bear-human debates. And just as bears learn to get along with humans and to count on their garbage, those same humans neaten up their act and get into recycling. (Not even the mightiest bear can muzzle open a flattened can!)

But whatever human civilization does to alter the backwoods lifestyle, the Goodbears hold a basic belief: when a door closes, a window opens. They would adjust. Meanwhile, Serena Goodbear taught her cubs the rudiments of coexisting with that other mostly upright species: *Homo sapiens:*

Try not to scare them (no telling what a spooked human will do) ❖ Be tolerant of the young ones ❖ Tippytoe around the nasty ones ❖ Search out the messy ones and become their garbage collectors ❖ Give them a wide berth on trails ❖ Hide from those who shoulder rifles ❖ Pretend to be afraid of noise, so they'll think they're safe when they clang their pans or toot their trumpets ❖ Don't visit the same humans more than once (or you may be targeted as a "nuisance") ❖ Don't burglarize their homes, dig up their gardens, shred their convertibles, or chug the contents of their hummingbird-feeders . . . unless, of course, you're starving, and then all rules of peaceful coexistence go out the cabin window (as you go in it)!

**When a door closes,
look for an open window.**

When a door closes,
look for an open window.

Jane Thomas Noland is a writer, humorist, and books editor. She and her daughter, Mimi Noland, are authors of *Bearables*, Parables of Bear Wisdom for Everyday Living, a Bearables book, and the first in a series from CompCare Publishers. Jane Noland is the co-author of the classic meditation book *A Day at a Time* (now with a million copies in print); author of *Laugh It Off*, a book about the importance of humor and laughter in losing weight, also illustrated by her daughter, Mimi Noland; and co-author, with award-winning illustrator Ed Fischer, of the best-selling gift book *What's So Funny about Getting Old?* With high school counselor Dennis Nelson, she also wrote a Twelve Step guide for teenagers, *Young Winners' Way*. She is a Phi Beta Kappa graduate of Smith College and a former feature writer for the *Minneapolis Star-Tribune*. She and her husband, Richard, parents of two grown children, live in Wayzata, Minnesota.

Mimi Noland, creator of the famous bears, illustrated Kathleen Keating's *The Hug Therapy Book, Hug Therapy 2* (bears), and *The Love Therapy Book* (dragons). The two hug books together have sold more than 700,000 copies and have appeared in over twenty foreign editions. She is the co-author of *Bearables* and author-illustrator of *The Hug Therapy Book of Birthdays and Anniversaries* and of *I Never Saw the Sun Rise* (written at age fifteen under the pen name Joan Donlan). Her illustrations appear in another best seller, *An Elephant in the Living Room,* by Jill Hastings, Ph.D., and Marion Typpo, Ph.D. (All books mentioned above are from CompCare Publishers.) Mimi Noland, a Skidmore College graduate in psychology, with further training in law enforcement and animal science, is also a singer-songwriter. She owns and operates a horse farm in Maple Plain, Minnesota.

Other Gift Books from CompCare Publishers

Quantity   **Title**

_____   ***Bearables*** *Parables of Bear Wisdom for Everyday Living* by Jane and Mimi Noland. The first book of the best-selling Bearables Series! Order #298-2

_____   ***The Hug Therapy Book*** by Kathleen Keating, drawings by Mimi Noland. Hug for health, hug for happiness. Hugging is for everyone. Order #065-3

_____   ***Hug Therapy 2*** Become a master hug therapist with the special language of hugs from the author and illustrator of *The Hug Therapy Book*. Order #130-7

_____   ***What's So Funny about Getting Old?*** by Ed Fischer and Jane Thomas Noland. Best-selling book of cartoons and quips that has created a new comedy genre: elderhumor. Order #243-5

_____   ***Welcome to Club Mom*** by Leslie Lehr Spirson, drawings by Jack Lindstrom. A humorous and practical guide to pregnancy and the first year of motherhood. Order #255-9

_____   ***What's So Funny about Looking for a Job?*** by Scott Badler. The practical and very funny book for job hunters and those who love them. Order #365-2

Call toll-free 1-800-328-3330

(We accept •Visa •Mastercard •Discover •American Express)

CompCare® Publishers

3850 Annapolis Lane, Suite 100   Minneapolis, MN 55447-5443

612/559-4800   Fax 612/559-2415